Books are to be returned on or before
the last date below.

LIBREX—

Published by A & C Black Publishers Ltd
36 Soho Square, London W1D 3QY
www.acblack.com

First edition 2009

ISBN 978 0 7136 8687 6

Acknowledgements
Cover photograph © Alun Richardson
Inside photographs © Alun Richardson except p.6 Kristjan Maack
Illustrations by © George Manley, except p. 51 © Crown Copyright
(2008), the Met Office
Designed by James Watson
Commisioned by Robert Foss
Edited by Lucy Beevor

Typeset in 9pt on 10pt Din-Light by Margaret Brain, UK

Printed and bound in South China by C&C Offset Printing Co.

Mountain Walking and Trekking is the first book in the **Rucksack Guide** series and covers the skills required to become a competent mountain walker. For walkers, the 'real' adventure starts when you step off the paths and explore the parts of the map where only streams, crags and contour lines exist. This handy book can be kept in your rucksack and will help you to gain the experience to walk safely anywhere in the world.

The **Rucksack Guide** series tells you *what* to do in a situation, but it does not always explain *why*. If you would like more information behind the decisions in these books, go to *Mountaineering: The Essential Skills for Mountaineers and Climbers* by Alun Richardson (A&C Black, 2008).

For more about the author, his photographs and the mountaineering courses he runs go to:
www.alunrichardson.co.uk and
www.freedomphotographs.co.uk.

ACKNOWLEDGEMENTS

The ideas in this book are the culmination of 25 years mountaineering and time spent discussing techniques with inspirational climbers, Mountain Guides and instructors, in particular Dave Williams, Steve Lewis, Graeme Ettle, Bruce Goodlad, Eric Pirie, Trevor Massiah, Clive Hebblethwaite, John Taylor, Twid Turner, Louise Thomas and Pat Littlejohn.

Special thanks to Lesley Jones who supported me throughout; Clive Hebblethwaite and Twid Turner who chewed over many issues with me in a tent and supplied some photographs; friends who commented on the text, some even posing for photographs – Trevor Massiah, Bas Jongmans, Paul Donnithorne, Clive Hebblethwaite, Paul Donnithorne, Emma Alsford and Gareth Richardson; Rhiannon Richardson and Molly Jones for help with text and diagrams; George Manley for his excellent illustrations; Robert Foss and Lucy Beevor from A&C Black and the manufacturers who generously supported the photo shoots: DMM, Lyon Equipment, Mountain Equipment, Face West, Select Solar, Mammut and Fritschi.

Any of the opinions expressed in this book are mine and should not be associated with any of the above people, companies or organisations.

PREPARING FOR YOUR TREK

The secret to being safe in the mountains is to understand the environment and to be prepared for anything it can throw at you. Be independent and self-sufficient – we do not have the right to be rescued.

Plan your route Examine the map carefully. If the weather is poor and the route complicated, put bearings and distances on the map for key stages.

Let friends know of your destination Leave a map or route card with friends or family with your intended route. Inform the same people of when you return.

Carry the correct equipment There is no such thing as bad weather, only inappropriate clothing.

RUCKSACK ESSENTIALS FOR DAY WALKING

Map stored in a watertight case
Compass (optional GPS receiver)
Extra clothing
Extra food and water
First aid kit
LED Head torch (extra bulb/batteries)

Knife (or multi-use tool)
Sunglasses
Sunscreen
Water bottle
Whistle
Emergency survival bag

QUESTIONS TO ASK BEFORE SETTING OFF

- Have you packed your rucksack with the necessary items (Fig. 3, page 17)?
- Strong winds and poor visibility slow you down – are you protected from the worst weather?
- What route are you taking? In what general direction? Break your route down into smaller sections, creating a mental picture of the legs.
- How far is the walk? How long will it take?
- Can you shorten the walk if required?
- How steep is the terrain?
- What is the ground like – will it speed you up or slow you down?
- Are there any prominent features you will pass on the way e.g. streams, paths, buildings, valleys?
- Are you going round hills or over them?
- Are there any dangers (steep slopes, rivers, hidden cliffs)?

Trekking in the Alps

PACE
- Don't walk too fast – enjoy it!
- Start slowly and speed up.
- Keep something in reserve in case you need it.
- Walk for at least an hour before stopping for your first rest.

THE REST STEP
- Straighten your rear leg in between every step so that it is supported by bone and not muscle.
- Relax the muscles of the forward leg.

DOWNHILL
- Tighten your laces.
- Bend your knees and place each foot lightly.
- Don't completely straighten your leg.
- Use the thigh muscles to absorb the impact, and not the knees.
- Keep a measured pace and zigzag to shift the strain.

NEGOTIATING BOULDER SLOPES
Stand in the gaps between stones, rather than on top of them.

AVOIDING KNEE INJURIES

Maintain the strength of the muscles supporting the knees, especially the quadricepts, which take some of the load off our joints.

The massive choice of equipment available can make buying kit a nightmare. Borrow equipment at first, and when you do buy take your time; read the latest reviews from the 'experts'.

CHOOSING BOOTS

Boots must be well constructed, water resistant, have an aggressive tread pattern, a medium level of ankle support and, most importantly, a good resistance of the sole to lateral twisting. Use good, well-fitting socks.

Type of boot	Pros	Cons
Approach shoes/soft-fabric boots	• Fine for treks on simple tracks • Lighter and dry faster • Cheaper	• Don't handle well in rugged terrain or poor weather • Ankle support and lateral stiffness are often lacking
Leather boot	• Still the most popular choice with mountain walkers • Sturdy ankle support • Can handle poor weather and grassy slopes	• You require a good water proofing agent to care for them • Can be expensive
Gore-tex boots	• Light • Great in hot conditions	• Terrible water-proofing in wet, muddy conditions

Getting a good fit

- Put the boot on un-laced. Push your foot forwards until your toes hit the front; you should then be able to squeeze a finger down the back of the heel.
- Next, lace the boots properly by standing up to weight the foot, but not too tightly over the arch – the foot is very sensitive to pressure.
- A good fit is one where there is no pressure on your toes, you can wiggle them, there is no side-to-side movement of the foot and your heel does not lift.
- If in doubt, buy larger.
- Put both boots on and simulate uphill and downhill walking.
- Wear a loaded rucksack because this will alter the shape of your foot.
- Finally try male and female versions – you never know!

Caring for boots

Stuff wet boots loosely with newspaper and leave them to dry in a warm, but not hot, place. Apply waterproofing to clean boots a few days before it is needed, to allow it to soak in (avoid too much treatment as it can soften the leather).

Socks

- Socks should be snug with a smooth knit, good shape and elasticity, and made of wool or synthetic fibres to draw moisture away.
- A thin liner and a thicker sock will reduce the chance of blisters.
- A Gore-tex sock worn over a thin liner sock functions like a Gore-tex boot.
- Do not roll your socks over the top of your boots or tuck your trousers into them as grit gets into the boot more easily.

LOOKING AFTER YOUR FEET

- Wash and moisturise feet every day.
- Air feet regularly.
- Use powders or antiperspirant to keep them dry, reducing blisters.
- Cut nails by following the contour of the nail, so that the nail corner is visible.

BLISTERS

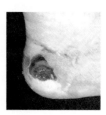

If your boots fit and they are laced correctly, you wear good socks and you look after your feet, you should never get blisters. If you feel a hot spot, act immediately. Always pop the blister, but do it neatly. Use a sterilised needle and pop several holes in the blister, press it flat and apply a small square of gauze to pad it. Hold the gauze in place with tape as it can be slippery. Plasters fall off, making a sticky mess at the first moment of perspiration.

MODIFYING BOOTS

Check how you walk by looking at the soles of an old pair of shoes:

- **Neutral** The wear is centralised to the ball of the foot and a small portion of the heel.
- **Overpronation ('flat feet')** There is too much movement of the foot and wear patterns show along the inside edges of your shoe.
- **Underpronation (supination)** The foot rolls outwards at the ankle, resulting in wear along the outer edges.

Orthotic foot beds, volume adjusters and stretching can increase comfort and ease painful rub points.

Poles help to protect your knees, make crossing streams easier, save you energy and generally speed you up – but only when they are correctly adjusted!

- Keep poles short – when standing on flat ground your hands should be below your navel.
- A rubber grip below the handle allows you to grasp the pole lower without having to adjust it.
- Don't use the hand loops (even cut them off!)
- Adjust the pole sections equally to maintain maximum strength.
- The basket helps to cope with mud.
- A flick lock, rather than a screw system, is more reliable and enables the poles to be cut shorter to fit inside your rucksack more easily.
- Two-, three- or four-section poles are available – the more sections there are the shorter the pole is when collapsed, but it means more joints and increases the cost (and weight) of the pole.
- Dry poles before collapsing, but do not oil the tubes – the joints may never lock firmly again!

DOWNSIDE OF TREKKING POLES

Poles do have downsides: they transfer the stresses to your elbows and shoulders, keep your hands full, increase total energy expenditure, and there is evidence that they prevent novices from learning essential balance. Use sparingly on simple walks, but when the going gets tough – especially downhill – they are invaluable.

CHOOSING GAITERS

- A good quality gaiter should be waterproof.
- Nylon is cheap, but not breathable, and canvas is durable, but stiff.
- Elastic or lace bindings under the boot are easy to use, but rubberised or cable straps last longer.
- Velcro closures are easier to use and keep water out, but a zippered closure with a good storm flap will work better.

Gaiters come in three designs:

1 **Low (stop tous)** Ankle-high and cooler, less able to keep rain and snow out, but my choice for most conditions.

2 **High** Calf-high and helpful when you are hiking on wet, muddy trails, wading through streams or crashing through vegetation.

3 **Full, over-the-boot gaiters** Useful when walking in very wet, boggy terrain, because they turn the boot into a Wellington. But they can be too warm, are expensive, and the rubber erodes easily, particularly the instep.

Fig. 1 Love them or hate them, gaiters help to keep ticks off your legs and grit, water and snow from getting inside your boots.

Wearing layers under your waterproofs traps heat more efficiently than one bulky item.

LAYERS

Type of layer	What to use
Next-to-the-skin	A performance fabric (polypropylene) that wicks perspiration away from your skin to the mid-layer
Mid-layer	A mid-weight synthetic fleece to hold in heat (avoid cotton)
Insulating layer	A thicker fleece
Waterproof layer	Also prevents the wind from cooling your body too much.

EXPERT TIP

Owen Samuel, BMG/IFMGA Guide
owenrichsamuel@hotmail.com

'When in the mountains, anything on your person that flaps in the wind or dangles past your knees will at some point slap you in the face or trip you over.'

WATERPROOF JACKETS

Waterproofs form the final layer and are crucial, not only for repelling rain but also reducing the wind chill. For most of us, the purchase of a jacket represents a significant investment and you get what you pay for. Look for lifetime guarantees. Waterproofs with zips to attach a fleece on the inside are rarely of any use. Smocks with a long zip are underrated – jackets are commonly either on, with the zip done up, or they are in a rucksack. However, smocks are more difficult to get on and off.

Materials

Waterproof fabrics are usually manufactured with coated fabrics or membrane fabrics. Large manu-facturers have their own cheaper, lower-performing brands that are often good value and perform well enough for most users.

A non-breathable coated jacket does not allow water in or out. When you exercise you get damp from sweat. In light rain you may find you are less damp without the jacket than with it! This type of jacket is, therefore, only suitable for short-term, non-strenuous use.

Breathable fabrics use either a microporous membrane laminated to a face fabric, where the pores in the coating are large enough to let water vapour pass through but small enough to keep water droplets out (Gore-tex), or a coating. Two types of breathable coating exist; microporous, which works like Gore-tex (Lowe Triplepoint), and hydrophilic (Sympatex), which relies on the chemical and molecular properties of water molecules. The more active you are, the more breathable the material must be. However, good ventilation and adjusting your layers to reduce sweating is just as important for keeping you dry.

Wired visor and large enough to fit over a helmet

Toggles tied at both ends

Taped seams

Good storm flap

Mesh-lined chest pocket

Short enough to give freedom of movement

Fig. 2 The parts of a good waterproof jacket

BUYING A JACKET

Identify the key activity you expect to use your jacket for and buy the most suitable and specific jacket, rather than making a compromised choice to suit a wider range of activities. Take any manufacturer's claims of staying dry in torrential rain with a pinch of salt as a fabric's breathability is always compromised when it is wet or dirty.

Fit

Your jacket should provide freedom of movement so try it on with the maximum layers you are likely to wear:

- Reach for the sky – are your wrists and belly exposed or does it pull at the waist and cuffs?
- Can you see your feet?
- It should not be too loose because you must build up a water vapour pressure difference between the inside and outside of the jacket to force water vapour out. Waist drawcords help to make your jacket fit more snugly.

Weight

The heavier a jacket is the more durable it is likely to be, but do you really need to add weight with a ski pass holder, pit zips or lots of pockets?

Length

- **Mid-length jackets** Protect the waist and thighs when walking, but can restrict movement.
- **Shorter jackets** Lighter and less bulky, fit under a harness and allow greater freedom of movement when scrambling or climbing, but they may expose your back when bending over.

Hood

- The attention to detail in the hood will tell you if the jacket is well designed.

- Hoods that roll away into a zipped pouch are rarely large enough and do not have a stiffened peak or wired visor – essential in the wind.

- A hood should be large enough to fit a hat or even a climbing helmet underneath it, but not so it flops down over your eyes or obscures your vision. Volume adjusters reduce the hood's size when you are not wearing a hat.

- Elastic drawcords on hoods, which are secured at both ends and 'lock' with a toggle that can be operated single-handedly, are the greatest advance in waterproofs. You no longer have to endure the cords flicking your face in windy conditions.

Zips and storm flaps

- Two-way zips allow you to increase ventilation, put the jacket on in a hurry and undo it to answer calls of nature!

- The zip is a weak point in combating the elements and it should have a Velcro storm flap to prevent water getting through.

- Uncovered, water-resistant zips on lightweight jackets work well when new, but they are not so durable and do not slide as easily.

- Pit zips (which vent the upper-arm area) can increase ventilation in extreme situations (you can achieve a similar effect by opening your cuffs, pockets and neck zip).

Pockets
Chest pockets should be mesh-lined, to improve ventilation, and large enough for a map (although this can be cut into smaller sections). An extra mesh pocket on the inside is useful for sunscreen or snacks etc. Avoid pockets below the waist if you regularly wear a harness.

SOFT SHELLS

This garment supposedly provides an outer and insulating layer in one. It is soft to the touch, water resistant, wind resistant, highly breathable and often stretchable. While not 100 per cent waterproof, a soft shell delivers twice the breathability. It does however take a long time to dry out when wet and you will then feel the cold more.

The decision to wear soft shells or conventional clothing depends on the activity. If rain is likely, a conventional waterproof jacket is important, but for aerobic activities in cold, dry, high-activity situations, soft shells may work well.

WATERPROOF OVER-TROUSERS

Often the discomfort these trousers can cause outweighs the protective factor: on a warm, wet day they make you sweat too much; on a cold, wet day you risk hypothermia without them. Carry a lightweight pair in summer and a heavy-duty pair of salopettes for winter conditions.

The most important thing is how easy they are to get on and off, plus how far you can lift your leg up in them. Full-length zips make them easier to remove and braces help to stop them sliding down.

CARING FOR WATERPROOFS

- Roll them up to keep the membrane flat inside your rucksack.
- Breathable fabrics are treated to make surface water bead up and roll off the garment. This keeps the fabric surface clear so that sweat and body heat can pass through from the inside. Over time the water-repellent treatment wears off and the garment becomes less effective. Try heating the material with a cool iron or in a tumble dryer, and when this no longer works treat the jacket with a reproofing product.
- Dirt and sweat can clog the pores of breathable materials. Most garments are machine washable, but avoid modern detergents, conditioners or softeners; use pure soap or a specialist cleaning product and check the care label.

CLOTHING ESSENTIALS

Up to 40 per cent of body heat is lost through your head, so carry a hat all year round, and a sun hat is vital. Gloves are also essential.

CORRECTLY ADJUSTED RUCKSACK

- The shoulder strap curves neatly over the shoulder when the hip belt is sitting correctly (Fig. 4, p. 19).
- The top of the hip should sit in the middle of the padded belt to transfer the load to the top of the buttocks.
- Tensioning straps link the top of the rucksack to the top of the shoulder straps and pull the rucksack closer to the back to improve stability. Release the straps when going downhill to keep the rucksack upright.
- Carry walking poles, tent poles, sleeping mats etc. on the compression straps.

RUCKSACK WEIGHT

Weight (litres)	Type of walking	Type of back
30	Day-long, summer walking	Simple padded back
50+	Multi-day walking between hostels and huts	Simple padded back usually in a variety of sizes
60–70	Camping	Usually adjustable back

EQUIPMENT

PACKING A RUCKSACK (Fig. 3)

- A rucksack is not waterproof. Store gear in watertight bags.
- Keep the load below your shoulders, close to your back and centred between your shoulder blades for balance.
- Do not carry an insulating mat across the top or bottom of the rucksack; it may get torn, wet and muddy.

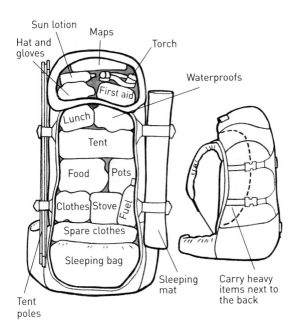

Fig. 3 Packing a rucksack

SELECTING A RUCKSACK

Choosing the correct rucksack will depend on what its intended main use is. The size is important, but so is volume adjustability; an overloaded small pack is as uncomfortable and unstable as a partly full one, especially if you have to hang gear outside.

Extendable lids

Extending lids increase the amount you can carry in the main compartment, but make the lid pocket difficult to use. They can also flop around when the sack is not full (fold the lid inside the sack and tuck the connecting straps away).

Comfort and fit

For small sacks and light loads a simple padded back is enough. Most larger sacks have a flat internal frame preventing the rucksack from losing its shape and transferring the weight to the top of your buttocks and your hips. Remove the wands from inside your new rucksack and get a friend to bend the struts to the shape of your back. Do not sit on your rucksack as you may bend the frame. Most adjustable harness systems allow the shoulder straps to move up and down the frame – if the back length is too long it will transfer the load to the collarbone. Tensioning straps link the top of the rucksack to the top of the shoulder straps and pull the rucksack closer to your back to improve stability. Release them when going downhill to keep the rucksack upright.

Compression straps

Compression straps reduce the rucksack's volume and hold the load closer to the wearer's back for stability. They are useful for carrying walking and tent poles, sleeping mats etc. Wand pockets at the base are also useful to attach poles.

Hip and waist belts

A padded hip-belt helps to redistribute a heavy load from your shoulders to your hips. The top of your hip should sit in the middle of the padded belt to transfer the load to the top of the buttocks.

Pockets

If the rucksack has a large lid pocket, side pockets are unnecessary; they get in the way and usually prevent the usage of compression straps. Bellowed or removable side pockets are a good compromise if you are a side pocket fan.

Zips

Rucksacks with zips give easier access to your gear, and are ideal for trekking where unpacking and packing is a regular occurrence. However, zips do break; take the strain off them with compression straps.

Head clearance

If you regularly wear a helmet, ensure the rucksack does not prevent you from looking up.

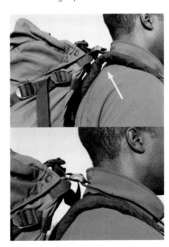

Fig. 4 On a correctly adjusted or sized rucksack the shoulder strap will curve neatly over the shoulder, as shown in the bottom picture.

- In an emergency you are the most important person. Next is everyone else around you. The casualty always comes last.
- Never put yourself or others in danger.
- Ensure that you have basic first aid training. Carry Dr Jim Duff's book *First Aid and Wilderness Medicine* (2007).

FIRST AID KIT
Pack everything in a small, clear Ortlieb watertight bag. A good first aid kit should:

- Stop serious bleeding
- Splint broken limbs
- Control pain
- Treat known chronic illnesses, allergies and skin conditions.

EXPERT TIP

Adam Gent, Rescue and Emergency Care Trainer (info@realfirstaid.co.uk www.realfirstaid.co.uk)

In an emergency you are the most important person – next is everyone else around you. The casualty always comes last. Never put yourself or others in danger. Keeping yourself and others alive is always the priority.

SMALL FIRST AID KIT

This first aid kit has been designed to cope with as much as possible using as little as possible.

Accident and casualty cards
Antihistamine cream
Antiseptic wipes
Aspirin and paracetamol
Cling film
Conforming and triangular bandage
Duct and transpore tape
Gloves
Glucose tablets
Ibuprofen
Iodine, non-adherent, wound and tegaderm dressings
Lancets
Pen torch
Plasters
Resuscitation face shield
Saline solution
Shears (strong scissors)
Steri-strips
Surgical blades
Tweezers
Waterproof pen

CARRYING AN INJURED PERSON

Placing two or more trekking poles in opposite directions behind the rucksacks of two people creates a good system for carrying an injured person off the hill. Wrap duct tape around the poles and pad them.

TENT DESIGNS

There are many variations on tent designs, ranging from ultra-lightweight to sturdier mountain designs, and in three- and four-season models (Fig. 5).

Dome tents

Dome tents provide a lot of sleeping space, but are not as stable as geodesic designs in strong winds.

Geodesic tents

These tents utilise four or five flexible poles in a self-supporting configuration, so they stand strong in the wind and provide generous interior headroom. Models with the poles running through the inner are roomier. They are also freestanding and my tent of choice.

Tunnel tents

Tunnel tents rely on two or three hoops. They are not freestanding and will collapse should the guying fail. They do not cope well in a storm or on snow. They are, however, lightweight.

Ultra-lightweight tents

Used for extended trekking in remote areas where you must carry everything yourself, ultra-lightweight tents usually have a single hoop or upright pole. They are not freestanding and may be unstable in high winds.

Single skin tents

These tents are usually made from one layer of breathable material. They are lightweight and quieter in strong winds, but are expensive, and the breathability depends on how warm it gets inside. If your sleeping bags are efficient you may find frost on the inside during cold nights. They are not as warm as double skin tents.

Fig. 5a Tunnel Geodesic large Dragonfly 2 X T (Mountain Equipment)

Fig. 5b Geodesic Hielo (Mountain Equipment)

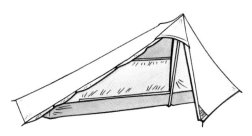

Fig. 5c Lightweight All Ultralight (Mountain Equipment)

MAKING YOUR CHOICE

The perfect mountain tent is spacious yet small, lightweight yet rugged, waterproof yet without a flammable coating. Consider the following:

- Your tent must be able to withstand the harshest conditions you might encounter.

- Cheap tents are great for non-serious camping, but won't withstand the stresses of a serious trip. UV resistance is poor, although you can enhance it with a spray coating.

- Three-season models are lighter and not as sturdily constructed. They often have netting that allows the elements to blow through. Four-season tents are 10–20 per cent heavier (typically due to extra poles), but are tougher in snowstorms, and the fly sheet extends to ground level.

- Ensure you compare like with like as manufacturers include different things in their weights.

- Freestanding tents can be easily moved to shake out debris. Very lightweight tents are rarely freestanding.

- Silicone-coated nylon is more expensive than polyester, but is lighter, more durable and more water repellent. Choose it for ground and fly sheets.

- Aluminium poles are much more reliable than fibreglass.

- Tent seams must be sealed.

- Capacity ratings are optimistic. A two-person tent is a tight squeeze for two large adults and their gear.

- Look for large storage pockets.

- Look for efficient venting – to reduce condensation – and mosquito netting.

- Think about the entrances for cooking and storage capacity. Leave rucksacks outside in a waterpoof bag if the porch is small.

PITCHING A TENT

- Practice erecting the tent before you leave.
- Colour-code the poles and sleeves for easier identification.
- Use strong tent pegs.
- Close the doors when erecting the tent to ensure correct tensioning.
- Push the poles, rather than pull them, through the sleeves.
- In strong winds, put a heavy item inside the tent when erecting or dismantling to prevent it from blowing away.
- If your tent sags after rain do not re-tension the guy lines, because it may shrink and rip as it dries out.
- When collapsing, disassemble the poles from the centre to stretch the elastic cord evenly.

CHOOSING A CAMPSITE

For camping on snow see *Rucksack Guide: Mountaineering in remote areas of the world* (A&C Black, 2009).

- Ensure the ground is well drained, sheltered and not easily damaged.
- Use a protective groundsheet on stony ground.
- Avoid cold low spots and pitch the entrance away from the prevailing wind.
- Camp more than 50m from water sources (water attracts mosquitoes and midges, and rivers can flood suddenly in heavy rain).
- Do not dig drainage channels.
- Hang food 100m from your tent and leave nothing aromatic inside it.

SURVIVING WITHOUT A TENT

It would be foolish to venture into the mountains without shelter, even in summer.

Foil blankets

These are a waste of time as they flap around and do not keep out the elements.

Plastic/foil bivouac (bivvy) bags

These are lightweight, and they do not let water in, but they also can't let water out. They are, however, excellent for simple day walks.

Waterproof/breathable bivvy bags

Breathable bivvy bags are best for extended use, when combined with a sleeping bag. However, they are too expensive to keep just for emergencies. Ensure the bivvy bag is large enough for a sleeping bag to expand fully. Gore-tex Exchange material is more permeable than standard Nexus Goretex. Hooped versions are heavy – a single skin tent is possibly better.

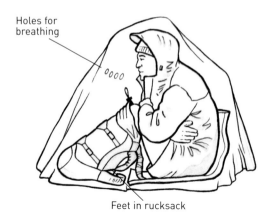

Holes for breathing

Feet in rucksack

Fig. 6 Using an orange plastic bivvy bag – pull it over your head and punch a few breathing holes in it.

***Fig. 7** A group shelter is a must for serious walkers.*

Sleeping bag covers
Protect your sleeping bag in damp conditions, and do not use it for sleeping outside in the rain.

Blizzard bags
Part bivvy bag, part sleeping bag, a blizzard bag is a lightweight alternative to a breathable cover and a sleeping bag. They are worth considering if you are somewhere where a plastic bag will not do. Blizzard bags are also available for one, two or three people.

Group shelters
A group shelter very quickly provides warmth and can be used for anything from simple lunch stops to more serious situations. Available for two or more people. Sit together on your rucksacks and pull the shelter over the top of you. Group shelters are windproof, but not completely waterproof.

Tent fly sheets
They are worth considering if you are on a budget, as they can do the same job as a group shelter and are waterproof (although condensation can be a problem). However, tent fly sheets are not lightweight enough or the right shape to be used without poles.

STAYING WARM IN A SLEEPING BAG

A sleeping bag should:

- Be long enough
- Be lightweight
- Be easily compressible
- Have a hood
- Have a full-length zip
- Have a neck/zip baffle
- Be warm enough for the coldest expected temperatures.

Let the sleeping bag 'loft' up and use an insulating mat. Exercise and eat something before getting into your bag to create more heat. Fill your Nalgene water bottle with hot water and take it to bed.

DOWN STRENGTH

The best bags have 95 per cent goose down with 5 per cent chopped feathers. The down's 'fill power' measures how much space a set sample of down occupies in cubic inches, and hence how much insulation it provides for its weight. For example, a 30g (1oz) sample of down with a fill power of 600+ occupies a minimum of 600 cubic inches. Therefore, the higher the fill power, the better the performance of the bag. A 550 fill power is used in mid-range bags; anything over 650 is excellent. (These figures are used in the European fill power test; in the US the figures are higher, but mean the same.)

CHOOSING A SLEEPING BAG

Consider the following when choosing a sleeping bag:

- **Mummy-style** bags insulate more because there are less interior dead areas, but they can be constricting. If you camp only in warm places, a rectangular bag is more comfortable.

- There are two main methods of constructing sleeping bags – 'stitch-' or 'sewn-through' and 'box wall'. **Sewn-through** bags are colder than **box wall** construction, but are cheaper.

  - **Down-filled** bags are lighter, compress better and last longer than synthetic versions. The down oils help quick recovery and dry as rapidly as synthetic materials. However down is more expensive and requires specialist cleaning.

  - **Synthetic** bags are cheaper and provide some insulation, even when wet. They dry out fairly quickly and are non-allergenic, but are heavier and bulkier. They lose their lofting ability more quickly due to constant compression when packed away.

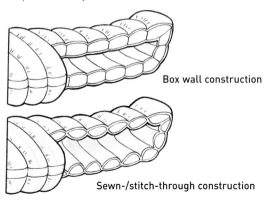

Box wall construction

Sewn-/stitch-through construction

Fig. 8 *Box and sewn-through construction of sleeping bags*

CARING FOR YOUR SLEEPING BAG

- Never leave your sleeping bag damp. Air-dry it every day and after every trip.
- Stretch it out on a bed or in a dry room until you're sure it's dry.
- Leave it loosely packed to prevent the breakdown of the filling.
- Avoid washing a down sleeping bag as it removes the oils – if necessary, use a small amount of down soap, a gentle cycle and rinse well.
- Take care when handling a wet bag – the shell and the baffles can rip.
- Do not separate the down by hand, but use a tumble drier with several tennis balls.

Insulating mats

When you lie in your sleeping bag, you are compressing the insulation. You will therefore require a reliable buffer between your bag and the ground. An air mattress is comfortable, but will not insulate you.

INSULATING MATS: PROS AND CONS

Type of mat	Pros	Cons
Closed-cell foam	• This mat is made from dense foam filled with closed air cells • Cheap • Durable • Non-absorbent • Insulate well, depending on thickness • Will not deflate	• Stiff (to make it easier to fold, strap to your rucksack, cut it into convenient strips and then stitch/tape them back together. • Uncomfortable

Self-inflating	• Expensive • Very comfortable • Insulate well • Compact when rolled up	• Heavy • Can be punctured, but are repairable (with a proper repair kit) • Your feet get cold when using a shorter vesion • The surface can be slippery and you can slide off during the night
Down-filled	• The highest degree of insulation and confort available without the bulk or weight	• The most expensive • Unreliable when used heavily

Fig. 9 A Gore-tex bivvy bag is essential for extended camping or bivvying in damp conditions. It also makes your sleeping bag warmer.

USING STOVES

- The size and material of your pan and how sheltered you are affects the cooking time.
- Clean and maintain the stove.
- Keep the fuel warm and filter it before use.
- Use a lid, windscreen and a reflective base, and consider a heat exchanger on longer trips.

CHOOSING A STOVE

	Pros	Cons
Aluminium	• Lightweight	• Dents easily
Stainless steel	• Durable	• Heavy • Can scorch the food
Titanium	• Lightweight	• Expensive

THE DUTCH OVEN

To conserve fuel, bring the food to the boil for approximately 15–30 seconds with a lid on. Turn off the stove and keep the pot hot with insulation for around 10–15 minutes.

Cooking in tents

- Always start the stove outside the tent.
- Have a wet cloth ready to smother the flames.
- Check the vestibule is large enough to allow you to cook there.
- Place the stove on a thin piece of wood in a tent.
- Ventilate, because carbon monoxide sinks.
- Put the stove outside of the tent when you have finished cooking.

FUEL: PROS AND CONS

Type of fuel	Pros	Cons
Butane, Propane or Isobutane blend	• Convenient, clean and easy to light • Burns hot immediately and does not require priming • Easily adjusted for simmering and cannot easily spill	• Expensive • You must carry and dispose of the canisters • Isobutane works better in cold conditions
Kerosene	• Inexpensive • Easy to find throughout the world • Has a high heat output	• Does not ignite easily • Smells and burns dirty • Spilled fuel evaporates slowly • Requires priming and it tends to gum up stove parts
Alcohol	• Renewable fuel resource with low volatility, that burns silently • The stoves have fewer moving parts, decreasing the chance of breakdown	• Have lower heat output • Perform poorly in the cold • Require more fuel, which can be hard to find
White gas (pure petrol)	• Inexpensive • Clean and easy to light • Spilled fuel evaporates quickly	• Spilled fuel can also ignite quickly • Requires stove fuel to prime it • Difficult to find in third world countries
Unleaded petrol	• Inexpensive • Easy to find throughout the world • An attractive option for travelling in remote areas, but ensure the stove is easily maintained	• Unleaded petrol burns dirty/sooty • Can lead to frequent blockage of the stove jet

MAINTAINING WATER LEVELS

Staying warm not only depends on clothing, but also on your water and energy levels.

- Eat a good breakfast and keep your energy levels up by eating small amounts of food (e.g. grain bars, dried fruit, bananas, peanut butter sandwiches) every 30 minutes or so.

- Smoking reduces peripheral circulation and can increase the chances of cold extremities.

- A five per cent drop in hydration levels can reduce performance by up to fifty per cent.

- Drink plenty two hours before going out, and a lot when you return. Water intake in hot environments should be about 2–3l a day.

- Hydration bladders are great, but are expensive, freeze in the cold and can tempt you to finish all your water too quickly.

- A warm drink is only psychologically different to a cold one (the energy content keeps you warm, not the heat).

EARLY SIGNS OF DEHYDRATION

- Headache
- Light-headedness
- Lethargy
- A vague feeling of being unwell.

DRINKING FROM STREAMS

- Water from glaciers should be avoided because of the tiny mineral particles.
- Water from springs, wells and long-term ground water is usually pure and wholesome.
- The Mountaineering Council of Scotland states that water from mountain streams in the UK can be consumed untreated if it is well away from human habitation, but avoid oily covered peat sources.

ENERGY AND REHYDRATION DRINKS

High glucose 'energy' drinks are not suitable for rehydration, because they slow down stomach emptying. Instead, drink water. Artificial sweeteners also dehydrate, because they draw fluid from the large intestine. Conversely, small amounts of salts, especially sodium and potassium, in a drink allow fluid to empty quickly from the stomach, promote absorption from the small intestine and thereby encourage hydration.

Isotonic sports drinks (in balance with the body's salts) or, even better, hypotonic (lower than the body's salts), with a carbohydrate level (complex glucose not pure glucose) of approximately six per cent, are emptied from the stomach at a rate similar to water. They may be beneficial if you are walking for a few hours or more and cannot eat.

MAKE YOUR OWN REHYDRATION DRINK

It is easy to make 1l of sports drink at a fraction of the price, also avoiding using plastic bottles:

- Isotonic – 500ml of unsweetened fruit juice and 500ml of water
- Hypotonic – 100ml of squash, 900ml of water and a pinch of salt.

HEAT FROM THE SUN

The weather is a massively complex subject, but despite the complexity of the global weather system, patterns exist that allow us to identify and predict common types of weather behaviour. For a detailed explanation of weather see *Mountaineering* (A&C Black, 2008).

On large scales regions closer to the Equator receive more heat from the Sun than those closer to the poles. On local scales differing surfaces absorb or reflect heat, e.g. snow reflects 90 per cent of incoming heat while dark green trees absorb the most. Without this uneven heating the world would be surrounded in an amorphous mass of weather. This differential heating causes local weather effects and, more importantly, global weather changes. To further complicate things the tilt of the Earth exposes regions of the Earth to the Sun at different times of the year, creating our seasons.

The heating of Earth causes warm air to rise, cool and fall. On a small scale the rising air causes things like coastal breezes. On a global scale the warming of the Earth and sea drives three large cyclical 'cells' of rising and falling air – The Hadley, Ferrel and Polar cells (Fig. 14, p. 41). It is at the boundaries between these differing 'global scale' masses of air that our dramatic weather systems are born. These localised and global weather patterns are separate entities, but affect each other to create chaos.

AIR PRESSURE

Rising warm air and denser, sinking cold air result in lower and higher pressure air masses or air systems. A lot of air above us is called **high pressure** and a small amount of air above us is called **low pressure**.

HOW ARE CLOUDS FORMED? (Fig. 11)

Warm, moist rising air cools and water vapour turns into water droplets forming clouds, and eventually rain. On a weather chart, the part of the Earth that the air mass is moving/circulating over tells you how much moisture it has (potential rain) and whether the air is cold or warm e.g. an air mass approaching from the southwest is moist and warm, from the northeast it is colder and drier.

***Fig. 10** A cumulonimbus cloud is created by warm air rising, often with devastating results.*

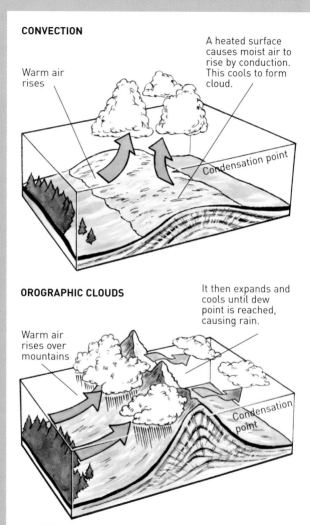

CONVECTION

Warm air rises

A heated surface causes moist air to rise by conduction. This cools to form cloud.

Condensation point

OROGRAPHIC CLOUDS

It then expands and cools until dew point is reached, causing rain.

Warm air rises over mountains

Condensation point

Fig. 11 Local level formation of clouds

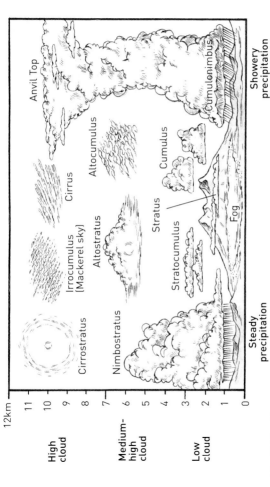

Fig. 12 Cloud types

HOW IS RAIN FORMED?

As air rises the pressure drops and the density decreases, meaning clouds can form. If they contain enough moisture it rains.

Local level generation

- **Convectional rainfall**
  Heating from below causes the warm, moist air to rise.
- **Orographic or relief rainfall**
  Air is forced to rise over the land and cools.

Global level generation

- **Frontal rainfall**
  When a mass of warm air meets a mass of cold air the warm air is forced up over the boundary (front) of cold air resulting in cooling and, hence, clouds.

Fig. 13 *Beware: heavy rain can cause flooding and make rivers that may fall in your path difficult to pass. If in doubt, rope up.*

To understand why we get large weather systems and frontal lifting we must examine the global circulation of air.

EASTERLIES AND WESTERLIES

In the northern hemisphere warm air rises at the Equator, moves northwards, cools at the poles, sinks and returns southwards. However, because the Earth is spinning the air is deflected to the right (westwards) of its direction of flow by the Coriolis Effect. This means that in the Polar and Hadley cells the air returning to the Equator at ground level is moving westwards to form the '**easterlies**'.

The gap between the Hadley and Polar cells is the Ferrel cell and, unlike the other cells, it is not a distinct cell (it is thermally inactive). Because it is an indistinct mass of air, the Ferrel cell is affected more by the general circulation of air around the world than the Coriolis Effect and the air is moving eastwards forming the '**westerlies**'.

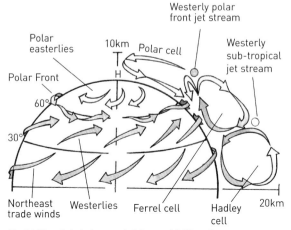

Fig 14 *The global picture of rising and falling air*

WEATHER

THE POLAR FRONT

At the boundary (front) between the Polar and Ferrel cells a sharp gradient in temperature occurs – **the polar front**. This creates a large pressure difference forcing air to move eastward with the circulation of the Earth. This air, known as the polar front jet stream, is very fast and it has to keep up with air circulating at the Equator. The polar front is not static and meanders and disappears, indicated by the jet stream. In winter, the polar front shifts south, bringing cold air to temperate latitudes. In the summer it moves north allowing warmer air to move northwest.

The high winds at altitude – the **easterly jet streams** – are created at the boundary between the Polar and Ferrel cells, formed by temperature differences in the upper atmosphere between the cold polar air and the warm tropical air. The spinning of the Earth and the relief of the land cause turbulence in the boundary between the easterlies and westerlies, which follow a forever-changing wave pattern around Earth (Fig. 15). If you want to see what is happening to our weather go to www.metoffice.co.uk to see interactive forecasts showing the movement of the jet stream, because it is at this boundary that depressions are formed.

WIND DIRECTION

A westerly wind comes in from the west and an easterly wind comes in from the east.

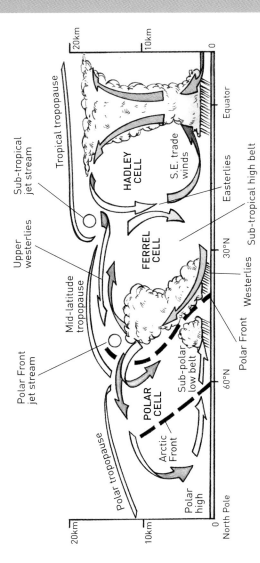

Fig. 15 *The polar front – the troposphere is the lowest of the Earth's atmospheric layers, where all of what we call 'weather' occurs.*

WEATHER

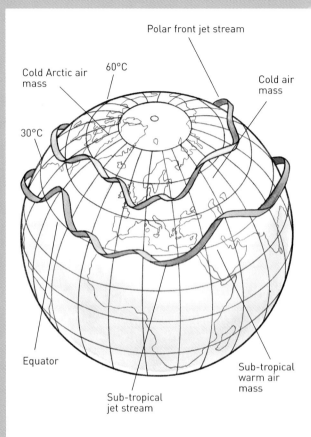

Polar front jet stream

Cold Arctic air mass

60°C

Cold air mass

30°C

Equator

Sub-tropical jet stream

Sub-tropical warm air mass

Fig. 16 *The jet stream is a good indicator of the polar front's position. The polar front is not the only boundary between air masses that exists, but it is the one that affects the UK, Northern US and Canada the most. Go to www.metoffice.co.uk to see interactive forecasts that show the movement of the jet stream and its associated fronts.*

DEPRESSIONS

The movement of the atmosphere, the effect of mountain chains and the warming of the sea creates great kinks in the polar front (Rossby waves – Fig. 15) that migrate from west to east and carry the high and low pressure areas generated by the localised warming of the Earth. As the warmer air rises up over the denser, colder air, the colder air rushes in to fill the void and the wave eventually closes up and disappears.

This is the formation and destruction of a **depression** – also called a **low-pressure system** – something, which is constantly happening at all times along the polar front. The latitude of the US/Canada and Britain is such that they are frequently under the polar front, explaining our characteristic unsettled weather!

The warm air, which occupies the segment of the ripple pushing up into the boundary, is moving slightly to the east. The surrounding cold air is moving slightly to the west, resulting in an anticlockwise rotation around the kink.

- A **depression** (low) is an area of low pressure and brings unsettled weather, because the air is rising and cooling.

- The deeper the depression (lower the air pressure), the more unsettled and windy the weather is.

- The amount of rain depends on the amount of moisture, which depends on whether it has travelled over dry land or the sea and where it is headed.

- The cloud and precipitation is not uniformly distributed around a depression.

- The most significant precipitation occurs along the fronts.

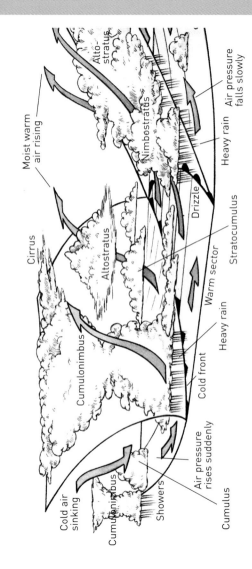

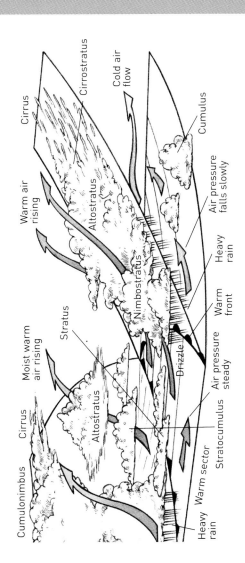

Fig. 17 A typical depression and associated fronts

- The leading edge of the warm area is the **warm front**.
- The back of the kink is the **cold front**.
- A front describes the condition of the air behind it.
- At any front there is invariably rainfall as warm air rises above cold.
- Cold fronts are faster moving (which is why depressions eventually die out) and bring shorter, but significantly heavier, rainfall.
- The warm sector inbetween is invariably warmer and drier.
- An **occluded front** occurs when a cold front catches up and overtakes a warm front. This causes the warm air to be undercut and elevated from the surface.

Fig. 18 A temperature inversion occurs when there is warmer air above and colder air below.

TYPES OF FRONTAL WEATHER

Type of front	Weather
Warm front	• Temperatures start to rise and the pressure steadily falls.
	• Thin, high-level cirrus clouds – up to 1000km ahead of the surface position – to low, dense stratus clouds.
	• Rain can extend 160–320km ahead of the front.
In the warm sector (after the passage of the front)	• Rise in temperature, a veer in the wind and pressure stabilises.
	• Amount of cloud falls as it begins to thin out.
	• Rain stops and the weather is generally fine, with a little stratus or stratocumulus.
Cold front	• Pressure and temperature falls increasingly rapidly, but pressure rises steadily when the cold front passes over.
	• Large, towering cumulonimbus clouds develop producing heavy downpours of rain and fierce squalls, sometimes with thunder.
After the cold front	• Heavy rain decreases as cumulonimbus clouds move away.
	• Barometric pressure continues to rise steadily.
	• Showers may occur, but it is generally fine and cool.
Occluded front	• Similar to cold front, but the rain belt is narrow.

Outside of a depression warm air is cooling and falling over a large area, creating areas of slow-moving high pressure called **anticyclones**.

Anticyclones spread outwards in a clockwise direction in the northern hemisphere and anti-clockwise in the southern hemisphere.

If rising air cools and forms clouds, sinking air warms and inhibits cloud formation. Hence anti-cyclones usually bring prolonged warm, dry, sometimes cloudless or hazy weather in the summer.

WEATHER FORMED BY ANTICYCLONES
Over land The sky is usually clear, which – during summer – means long, sunny days and clear nights. In winter, the longer nights mean that temperatures fall lower, with frost forming, which may persist all day. The fall in temper-ature overnight and light winds can create fog.

Over sea (picking up moisture) Varies from fine and sunny to overcast cloud, possible drizzle and maybe fog. If the moist air is pushed up over mountains, it can rain (occurs most often during spring and is least frequent in autumn).

PREDICTING THE MOVEMENT OF DEPRESSIONS
Depressions occur in 'families', which migrate east-wards along the polar front until a ridge of high pressure builds up to block any further depressions from advancing.

- Future movement of a depression is often an extension of its previous track.
- Depressions tend to move from areas of increasing pressure to areas of decreasing pressure.

- The centre of the depression will move parallel to the isobars in the warm sector.
- Depressions tend to move around large, stationary high pressure areas.
- A depression with an occluded front tends to move to the left of its track.

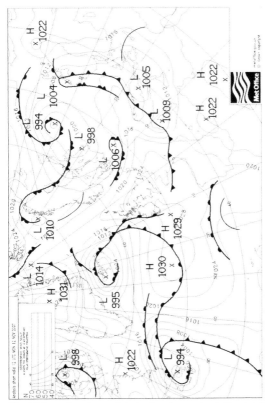

Fig. 19 A weather (synoptic) chart – always check the date!
© Crown Copyright (2008), the Met Office

READING WEATHER CHARTS

Symbol	Weather
Isobars	Lines joining areas of equal pressure
High pressure or anticyclone	Widely spaced isobars, where pressure is higher than surrounding areas.
Low pressure or depression	A thumb print. Winds blow anticlockwise. Isobars close together means strong winds, wider apart means light winds.
Trough	An elongated extension of an area of low pressure. Brings similar weather to depressions.
Ridge	An elongated extension of an area of high pressure. Brings similar weather to anticyclones.
Col	An area of slack pressure between two weather systems.
Cold front	Blue triangles. The side of the front that has the 'triangles' indicates the direction in which the front is moving.
Warm front	Red semi-circles. The side of the front that has the 'humps' indicates the direction in which the front is moving.
Occluded front	Has both triangles and bumps

Large cumulonimbus thunderclouds generate energy as the air rises and falls within the cloud. Lightning is a large electrical spark caused by the movement of electrons in cumulonimbus clouds and thunder is the expansion of air caused by extreme heat. Ninety per cent of lightning travels from cloud to cloud (sheet lightning), meaning that 10 per cent is coming earthwards!

LIGHTNING

Lightning can strike up to 50km from its origin. To determine the distance in km between the lightning strike hit and your position, count the number of seconds between the lightning flash and the thunder, and divide by three.

AVOIDING LIGHTNING STRIKES (Fig. 21)

Direct lightning strikes are rare; you are more likely to be hit by a side flash or ground current as it arcs to find an easy way to ground.

Ground current pathways include cracks and crevices filled with water, wet rock, wet climbing ropes, root systems and cables along the ground. The current flows right through you if you are between a gap so taking shelter at the opening of a cave may be more hazardous than being out in the open.

- Get off the highest location.
- Stay away from taller trees and out of depressions, gullies and water.
- Avoid caves and overhangs unless they are dry and suitably large.
- If you cannot get down, remove metal objects, occupy as little area as possible and sit, crouch or stand on your pack with your hands and feet off the ground.

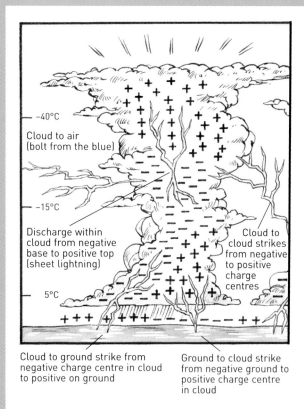

Fig. 20 *A thunderstorm and the formation of lightning*

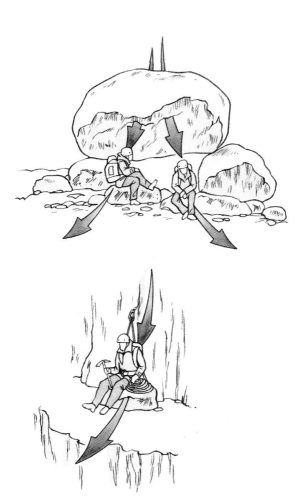

Fig. 21 *Unsafe places to shelter in a lightning storm*

CLOUD AND RAIN

There is little doubt that mountain ranges can dramatically influence global climate (the Canadian Rockies are known to generate Rossby Waves). At the local level, mountains force air to rise and consequently assist the formation of clouds and precipitation. Mountains therefore tend to have much wetter climates than the surrounding plains.

Most airflow in the Earth's atmosphere is orientated along east-west trends. Consequently, north-south orientated mountain ranges have the ability to influence the general circulation. Although some air is forced to rise over mountains, the eastward movement of large air masses are generally deflected by north-south orientated mountain chains, e.g. The Rocky Mountains deflect air to the north, which cools in the polar latitudes before returning south. The colder north-westerly wind influences the climates of the Canadian and US interiors, and winter temperatures are therefore exceedingly low.

IT GETS COOLER AS YOU GO HIGHER (LAPSE RATE)

The average temperatures on hills and mountains are much lower, the winters longer and summers much shorter.

Temperature usually falls with height at a set rate (lapse rate) depending on the humidity of the air – the average in the UK is 2°C per 300m.

TEMPERATURE INVERSIONS

As you ascend temperature usually decreases, but the opposite can occur. A **temperature inversion** is when there is warmer air above colder air. The most common formation is on still winter evenings when the ground – and the air near the ground – cool quickly, but as air is a poor heat conductor it does not mix with the warmer air above. This inversion only disappears the following morning, when the Sun heats up the ground.

LOCALISED WINDS

Mountains are windier places. Hills force air to rise, either when winds have to go over them or as they become heated by the Sun. As the air descends on the other (lee) side, it becomes compressed, dries and warms, sometimes enough to create a strong, gusty, dry wind. The term **Föhn** is often used as a generic term for a warm downslope wind, although it does have other local names around the world such as 'Chinook' (meaning snow eater) in Colorado, US.

Not all downslope winds are warm. Even when air warms as it descends it can still be cooler than the air it is displacing, which results in a biting cold wind. **Katabatic winds** occur when cold, dense air drains down a mountainside into the valley below (e.g. the 'Mistral' in France).

WIND CHILL

Wind chill is the apparent temperature felt on exposed skin due to the combination of air temperature and wind speed. The effect of wind chill is reduced if you cover up.

WIND CHILL

Wind speed (km/h)	Wind chill temperature (°C)							
	0	–5	–10	–15	–20	–25	–30	–35
10	–2	–7	–12	–17	–22	–27	–32	–38
20	–7	–13	–19	–25	–31	–37	–43	–50
30	–11	–17	–24	–31	–37	–44	–50	–57
40	–13	–20	–27	–34	–41	–48	–55	–62
50	–15	–22	–29	–36	–44	–51	–58	–66
60	–16	–23	–31	–38	–45	–53	–60	–68

Stay in touch
A tiny AM radio can pick up local stations, even in the wilderness.

Look at the sky
The shapes and movements of clouds typically foreshadow the arrival of warm fronts and cold fronts.

Get up early
If late-day storms become a pattern, rise early and cover as much ground as you can during better weather.

Altimeters
The barometer and thermometer on your altimeter watch can be used to monitor changes in the weather. In general, rising air pressure is a good sign; conversely, a rapid or significant drop in air pressure (e.g. decreasing at 2mbar an hour, or a 10mbar drop overnight for instance) is invariably a warning that bad weather may be on the way.

Fig. 22 *Moist air rising over the hills can create its own weather (North Wales).*

Navigation is easy to learn, but using the skills under stress is the tricky part.

Best large-scale map in the UK OS 1:25,000 Explorer (1cm represents 25,000cm or 250m on the ground, so 1km on the ground is 4cm on the map (grid lines every 4cm)). They all have the features a walker requires.

Best small-scale map OS 1:50,000 Landranger (1cm represents 500m on the ground, so 1km on the ground is 2cm on the map (grid lines every 2cm)). Better for route-planning and winter use.

Harvey 1:25,000 and 1:40,000 walkers' maps Map popular upland areas and long-distance paths. They place less stress on land ownership boundaries (which obscure OS maps in places) and are very clear.

MAPPING DIFFERENCES

- **Continental maps** of mountainous areas use shading to create a 3D effect.
- **Swiss maps** have the slopes facing north and west shaded lighter than those facing south and east.
- **Some French maps** have few grid lines and some Austrian maps have none at all.
- **The French Alps** have a 10m vertical interval that changes to 20m when you cross into Switzerland, Germany and Austria, sometimes on the same map! The magnetic variation is very small and is largely ignored.

BEWARE OF CHANGING MAPS

Most maps are accurate, but they only show the land at a particular point in time, when it was surveyed. Glaciers retreat, fences are moved and forests are planted.

LOOKING AFTER YOUR MAP

Weatherproof maps are heavy and more expensive. Instead:

- Remove the cover, cut the map into useable segments and laminate with clear plastic.
- Carry two maps; a laminated 1:25,000 cut-out of the area with standard approach/descent bearings and distances etc. annotated on the back, and a 1:50,000 of the whole area, kept as back up in your rucksack.
- Clear waterproof map cases can make it difficult to read the map and take bearings. Cheap ones can crack and leak; the best are made from a stretchy plastic e.g. Ortlieb.

DIGITAL MAPS

Software packages are cheap when compared to collecting the equivalent paper maps. You are able to:

- **View and print** maps at different scales over and over.
- **Draw** on the map or enter a series of grid references.
- **Calculate** the length and height profile of routes, with estimated times.
- **Share** routes with other users.
- **Link** with a compatible GPS and/or pocket PC, to programme your GPS with a route in advance; record a route on your GPS as you walk it and then download it to your home computer; and even view a map and route on a pocket PC while walking.
- **See** maps in 3D form with virtual 'walk-throughs' of your route.
- **Scan** in your own maps (e.g. Fugawi systems).

Maps contain a lot of information, but they cannot tell you what the terrain is like or how difficult it may be to walk on. Most maps are incredibly accurate, but they do only show the land when it was surveyed, so the more recent your map the more accurate it is.

When the image is taken from the globe and put on a flat sheet the lines of longitude are used as reference points (Fig. 23). Vertical lines are 'lines of longitude'; horizontal lines are 'lines of latitude'.

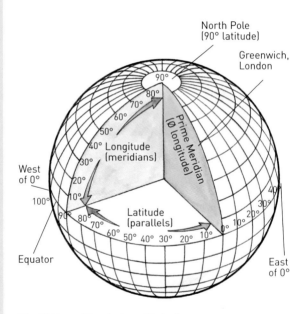

Fig. 23 Lines of longitude and latitude

The UK National Grid uses latitude and longitude to separate the country into easily map-able sections. Each square is 100km² and is given a two-letter code. It is then subdivided into 1km² grids, which is what you see on UK maps.

The Grid uses 49° North and 2° West (True North) as a starting point. The vertical grid lines are **'eastings'**; the horizontal grid lines are **'northings'**. Each grid square has a unique four-figure number – a grid reference – giving an accurate point of location. Further subdividing the grid square into 100m squares enables you to give a six-figure grid reference (Fig. 25).

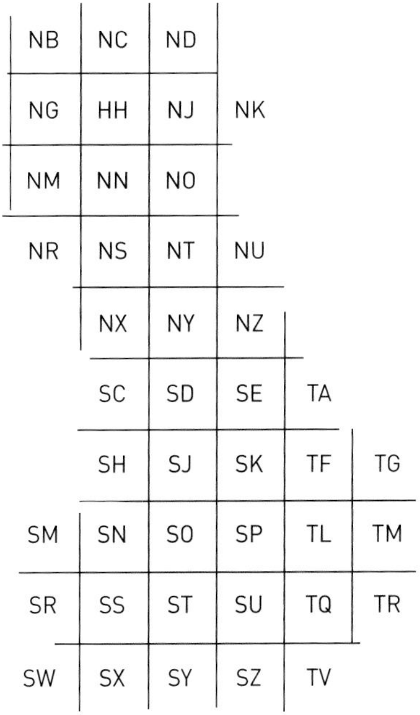

NB	NC	ND		
NG	HH	NJ	NK	
NM	NN	NO		
NR	NS	NT	NU	
	NX	NY	NZ	
	SC	SD	SE	TA
	SH	SJ	SK	TF	TG
SM	SN	SO	SP	TL	TM
SR	SS	ST	SU	TQ	TR
SW	SX	SY	SZ	TV

Fig. 24 The UK National Grid

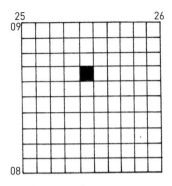

Fig. 25

Read along the eastings and then along the northings, e.g. 2508 is the four-figure grid reference for the 1km square. The six-figure grid reference for the marked square is 254086. To be truly accurate a grid reference should include the two letters of the 100km square before the numbers, identifying your location.

MEASURING DISTANCE

- Each grid square on an OS map represents 1km across and approximately 1.5km diagonally.
- Use the ruler on the side of your compass and do some simple maths, or use the romer (Fig. 26) to find distances.
- Remember that measuring distance on a map is an estimate, because it ignores the inconsistencies in the terrain.

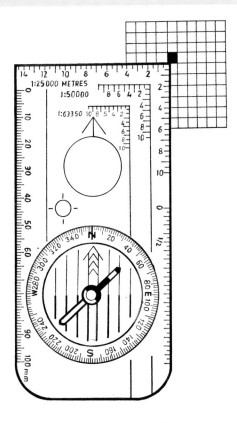

Fig. 26 *Using a romer scale to find a grid reference or to measure distance*

Contour lines are the thin orange or brown lines on a map with numbers. They show the shape and height above sea level of the land. A single contour line is at the same height along its length. There are four basic principles to reading them:

1 Contours close together represent steep land.

2 Contours wide apart represent flatter land.

3 Contours getting closer together towards the summit show a concave slope.

4 Contours getting wider towards the summit show a convex slope.

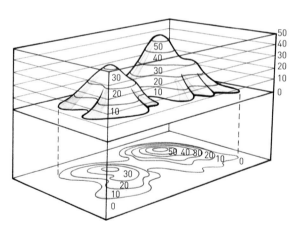

Fig. 27 The map key states the contour interval used (OS 1:25,000 maps show them 10m apart; Harvey's 1:25,000 maps show them 15m apart). Think of them as tide lines, left by the sea as the water level drops.

WHICH WAY IS UP?
Two signs tell us which way the slope runs: the numbers on the contour lines and all rivers join downhill (confluence).

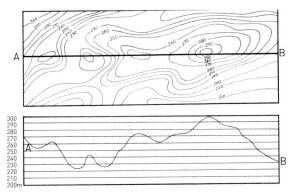

Fig. 28 *Sectional view of a map*

MISSING FEATURES

Contour lines can miss smaller features that appear on the ground. A 9m high feature can sit between 10m contour intervals and may not appear on the map, but if it exceeds the contour interval by 1m it is shown. If the feature is just below the contour line, then it may be shown as a dotted line.

MOUNTAIN FEATURES

Feature	Description
Basin	1) Area of fairly level ground surrounded, or nearly surrounded, by hills 2) Area drained by a river and its tributaries
Cwm/Cirque	Natural amphitheatre at the head of a valley
Col	Easily accessible depression between adjacent hills or mountain tops
Crest	1) Line on a range of hills 2) Top of a ridge from which the ground slopes down in opposite directions
Gorge	1) Narrow stream passage between steep rocky hills 2) Ravine with precipitous sides
Knoll/ring contour	Small, knob-like hill
Left/right bank	Bank of a river on the left/right, facing downstream
Plateau	Level elevated region
Re-entrant	Very small valley (maps usually show it as an/several indented contour line/s)
Spur	Ridge running out from a hill or mountain

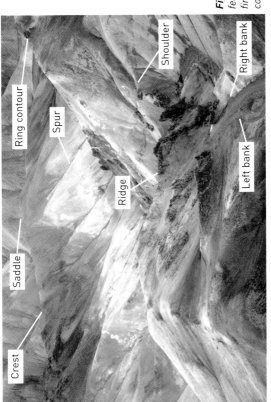

Fig. 29 Understanding features on a map is the first step to being a competent navigator.

Ring contour

Saddle

Crest

Spur

Ridge

Shoulder

Right bank

Left bank

NEGOTIATING SCREE SLOPES

A scree (talus) slope is broken rock that appears at the bottom of crags, mountain cliffs or valley shoulders, and varies from slopes consisting of small stones to large boulders. Aim to step on stable, larger rocks on boulder-strewn slopes. Scree with small rocks is easier to walk down than up as it slides with you. Walk independent lines or close together to avoid knocking stones on to those below you.

COMPASS TOGGLES

It is useful to carry toggles on your compass, which you can slide along to keep a record of the number of 100m walked.

In poor visibility a compass is vital:

- The best compasses are those with a long base plate and fluid to dampen the movement of the needle, e.g. Silva type 4.
- The needle is a magnet – keep it away from metal sources and objects; high-tension power lines up to 55m away; magnetic therapy bands on your wrist and even underwired bras!
- Keep your compass attached by a cord to an upper pocket of your jacket, or consider a pouch to keep the base plate in good condition.

BASE PLATES

If you break the base plate do not throw your compass away as you can get a replacement.

BUBBLES

You may find that after time, and if you go to altitude, bubbles appear in the housing. Do not worry, unless they affect the needle action.

The direction of travel arrow – Shows the direction that you want to travel along or the bearing you are taking.

The compass needle – Floats on liquid so it can rotate freely. The red end points to magnetic north.

Orienting lines – Move as the compass housing rotates to align with the eastings on a map. On some compasses half the lines are coloured red to indicate north.

The compass housing – Contains the magnetic needle and has the points of the compass printed on a circular, rotating bezel.

The index line – Fixed on the base plate and within the outer edge of the compass housing. It marks the bearing you set by rotating the compass housing.

Orienting arrow – Fixed within the compass housing, aligned to north.

The base plate – The compass's mounting, with a ruler for the measuring scale.

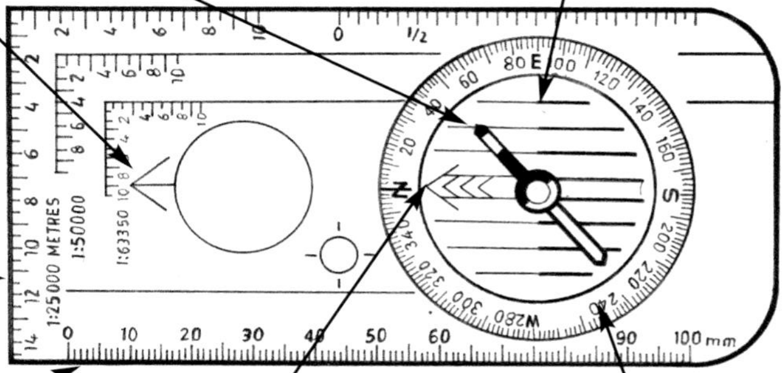

Romer/Compass scale – Displayed along the edge of the base plate so that you can measure distances on maps.

Fig. 30 The parts of a compass

GOING NORTH

- All maps are set from a line of longitude, where grid north lines up with true north.

- As one travels east or west from that line of longitude, magnetic north no longer lies perfectly with true north. Since the needle is a magnet it points to magnetic north (Fig. 31).

- The **magnetic variation** (declination in the US) is the difference between the two north's, depending on where you are in the world.

- The magnetic variation (which can be east or west of your position) between grid north and magnetic north is required for taking a bearing.

- The magnetic variation is normally given in the map margin, but do not forget to take into account the change from when the map was produced.

CORRECTING FOR MAGNETIC VARIATION WHEN TAKING A BEARING

From the map and applying it to the ground
When the variation is to the west (the situation in the UK) you must add degrees. When it is to the east, you must minus degrees.

From the ground and applying it to the map
When the variation is to the west (the situation in the UK) you must minus degrees. When it is to the east, you must add degrees.

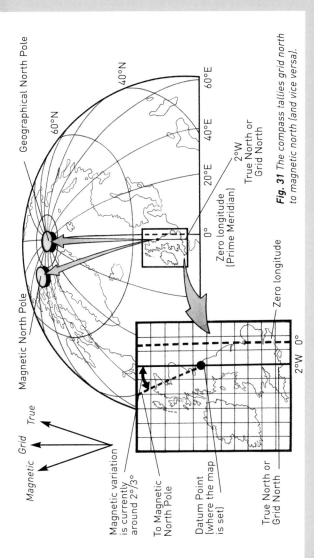

Fig. 31 The compass tallies grid north to magnetic north (and vice versa).

Geographical North Pole

60°N

40°N

60°E

40°E

20°E

2°W
True North or
Grid North

Zero longitude
(Prime Meridian)

Magnetic North Pole

True
Grid
Magnetic

Magnetic variation
is currently
around 2°/3°

To Magnetic
North Pole

Datum Point
(where the map
is set)

Zero longitude

2°W

0°

True North or
Grid North

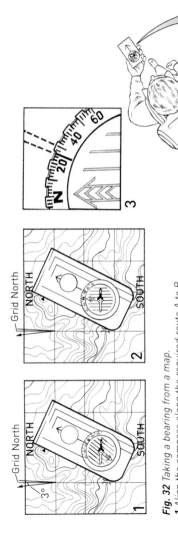

Fig. 32 Taking a bearing from a map.

1 Align the compass along the required route A to B.

2 Holding the compass firmly in place so as not to move it on the map, rotate the compass housing to align the orienting lines with north–south on the map.

3 Rotate the compass housing to compensate for magnetic variation.

4 Remove the compass from the map. Place the compass flat in the palm of your hand in front of you. Turn your whole body (not just the compass) until the needle is aligned with the north arrow and proceed, following the direction-of-travel arrow.

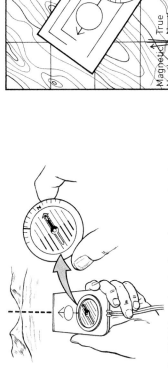

Fig. 33 *Taking a bearing from the ground to the map.*

1 Point the direction arrow at a feature you can clearly see.

2 Twist the compass housing until the north arrow is underneath the magnetic needle.

3 Remove the magnetic variation.

4 Place the compass on the map making sure the north arrow is parallel to the line of longitude and is pointing north.

5 Slide the compass into position so that the edge intersects either your position or the feature – whichever is known. (Ignore the magnetic needle now, it is always pointing north.)

6 Ensure the direction arrow is pointing away from your position or towards the feature.

Orientating the map requires you to identify features on the ground and then rotate the map until everything matches up. For example, you may be at a junction with paths diverging in different directions. Turn the map until it matches the directions of the paths. You now have the map orientated.

Use a compass when visibility is poor. Place the compass anywhere on the map in any position and simply turn the whole map (not the compass) until the north end of the magnetic compass needle points to the top (north) of the map, and is lined up with the grid lines (Fig. 34).

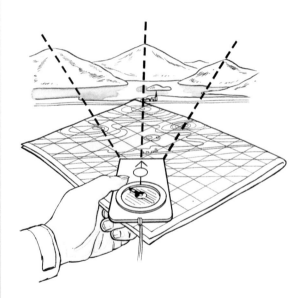

Fig. 34 *Set the map by rotating it until it matches the ground around you.*

Fig. 35 *Keep your maps at the top of your rucksack or in your pocket for easy access.*

READING THE GROUND

This is the skill of reducing ascent and descent by contouring, and avoiding obstacles with minimum effort and maximum speed. Practice reading the map. Select features on the map and identify them on the ground, and then find features on the ground and identify them on the map. Identify smaller and smaller features until the map comes alive.

Mental maps Create a mental picture of your route and 'tick off' features as you pass them. Break the route into smaller 'legs' so that your mental map is easier to store.

Hand-railing Follow a stream, wall, ridge or steep slope that will definitely lead you to your intended location (Fig. 41, p. 91).

Contouring Beware that when traversing a slope there is a tendency to lose height.

IDENTIFYING YOUR LOCATION

Even the best navigators do not always know exactly where they are in the mountains, but they have a strategy to find out.

From the map I think I am here on the map. If I am, then I must be able to see the following features identified from the map e.g. a steep slope in front and a ridge to the left. If I can't see them, I am not where I think I am.

From the ground I can see the following features e.g. a steep slope in front, a ridge to the left – where are they on the map? If I can find them I must be at this location.

From a compass bearing The mist clears and you can identify a peak or col. A bearing taken on it helps you to find your location.

Fig. 36 Reading the terrain and matching it to what is on your map is fundamental to good navigation.

From transit lines (Fig. 37) You may be descending a ridge and the mist clears. In the distance is the summit of an identifiable peak. Take a bearing on it: lay your compass on the map, with one of the long sides at the peak. Move the compass until the orienting lines in the housing are in line with the grid lines. You must be where the line crosses the ridge. Do not worry about magnetic variation unless it is more than just a few degrees.

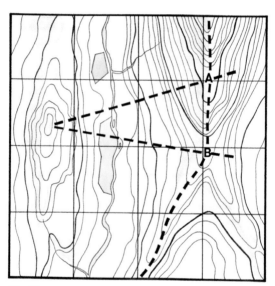

Fig. 37

From the slope aspect (Fig. 38) Useful when contouring a mountain, rather than going over it or following a plateau rim. To find your approximate position, point the compass in the direction of the fall line (the track a ball would take if you rolled it down the hill). Do not point your compass downhill. Transfer this bearing to your map. Like a transit, you must be close to where that line crosses your contouring route. (This method mainly eliminates only where you are not located).

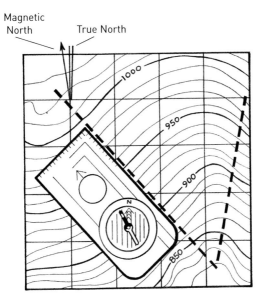

Fig. 38

How can we find how far we have walked when it is dark or misty?

Pacing
● Know how many paces you take for every 100m. Counting the strides on one leg means a smaller number to remember.
● Do not exaggerate, walk normally and keep a steady pace.
● On steep terrain, or in dense vegetation skip a pace or add a pace now and then rather than trying to maintain your standard pace.
● Most importantly, always relate the ground to your paces; if you reach an uphill section that is 200m away and you have only walked 150m according to your paces, then your pacing is wrong!
● Carry toggles on your compass that you can slide along to keep a record of the number of 100m walked.

Timing
Use the map to measure how far a route is and then, if you know how fast you are walking, you can work out how long it will take. At 4km/hr, which is an 'average' speed for most walkers with a light rucksack, it will take you 1.5 minutes to cover 100m, so a leg of 700m on flat ground should take you 10.5 minutes to walk (remember to account for the inconsistencies in the terrain). However when ground is uneven, correct your timings with Naismith's formula.

NAISMITH'S FORMULA
The Scottish climber, Naismith, created this simple formula which takes into account the changes in height while calculating speed over the ground:
Xkm/hr plus ½ hour for every 300m of ascent or 1 minute per 10m contour line.

On a descending slope it is assumed that you will be walking faster on shallow slopes, but slower on steeper descents. Therefore no adjustments are made for descents because it will even out over the day.

Horizontal distance (m)	Speed (km/h)				
	2	3	4	5	6
1000	30	20	15	12	10
900	27	18	13.5	10.8	9
800	24	16	12	9.6	8
700	21	14	10.5	8.4	7
600	18	12	9	7.2	6
500	15	10	7.5	6	5
400	12	8	6	4.8	4
300	9	6	4.5	3.6	3
200	6	4	3	2.4	2
100	3	2	1.5	1.2	1

Vertical height (m)	Time (mins/seconds)			
10	0.45	1.00	1.15	1.30
20	1.30	2.00	2.30	3.00
30	2.15	3.00	3.45	4.30
40	3.00	4.00	5.00	6.00
50	3.45	5.00	6.15	7.30

Fig. 39 Timing chart

A to B Distance 850m = 8 x 12 = 96 = 9.6 minutes. Round off to the nearest half minute = 9.5 minutes. Add 0.5 minute for the extra 50m = 10 minutes.

Height gain 130m (13 contours, including the one which encloses the 1,083 spot height), 1 minute for every 10m (or for every contour if using this map) = 13 minutes.

Total time from A to B: 10 + 13 = 23 minutes

TIMINGS

While timings are useful, do not rely on them to the exclusion of other more important things such as what the ground is doing underfoot – is it flat, uphill or downhill?

TAKING AND WALKING ON A BEARING

● Create a stable platform for the map by kneeling and using the front of your thigh as a table.

● If the weather is bad, move into a group shelter to take a bearing.

● In wet conditions use the long black lines marked inside the base-plate edge to line the edge of your compass accurately along the bearing on the map.

● After you have taken your bearing, hold the compass just above waist height with the direction of travel arrow pointing forward. Lock your elbow into your side and turn your whole body (not just the compass) to reach the required direction of travel.

● Following a bearing is laborious on routes longer than 250m. Instead, select a distant feature that is on the bearing, walk to it, check your direction of travel and set off again to a new object.

● Back bearings help to check that you are not following a parallel line. Turn and identify an object on the reverse bearing (match the white compass needle with the orienting arrow), walk and, after a while, turn and check the object is still on the same back bearing.

ERRORS
The most common error is walking off in the opposite direction, usually caused by:

- Placing the compass on the map, with the direction arrow pointing towards your location, not where you are heading.
- Lining up the north arrow along the grid lines, but pointing south.
- Holding the map upside down, but lining up the north arrow to the 'top' of the map – pointing south.

On occasion you will come across an unavoidable obstacle that takes you away from your bearing, e.g. a small lake or crevasses. You have two options, depending on visibility:

1 Leave a friend behind (use a head torch if it is dark). Walk around the obstacle, and when you have a back bearing that lines you up, stop and your friend can join you.

2 Walk a rectangle around the object. At the obstacle make a right-/left-angled 90° turn, walk X paces until you can walk around the obstruction, then turn left 90° and walk until you can turn 90° left again and return X paces. Now turn back to your original bearing. You should be along your original line of travel.

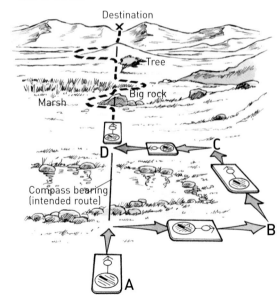

Fig. 40 Navigating around obstacles

BAD WEATHER
The mist is down, darkness has arrived, you know where you are and where you need to get to, but you cannot see the ground ahead. What do you do?

Plan your route
Break it down into shorter, more manageable legs.

Aim for obvious features
Such as a definite change in direction or steepness of a slope.

Hand-rails
Attempt to travel along them to maintain the correct direction (Fig. 41, p. 91).

Guess time, distance and direction
Then when you work it out accurately you'll spot if you make a mistake.

Take a bearing on the leg
Even pre-plan them and write them down if you are somewhere comfortable.

Calculate the time taken
4/5/6km hr plus 1 min/ contour.

Ground
What will it be like? Are you going uphill or downhill? Are there any identifiable features on the way?

Collecting features
Identify something that will tell you whether you have passed your navigation point.

Dangers
Are there any on the route e.g. a cliff, crevasse?

Strong wind
When battling a strong wind you will inevitably veer away.

HAND-RAILING, ATTACK POINT AND AIMING OFF

If the next place you want to go to is not easily identifiable, use the following techniques:

Attack points Navigate to something obvious or larger that is closer to your indistinct point.

Aiming off To find a path that crosses a wall or stream, do not navigate directly to it, but deliberately to one side of the wall or stream, following until you find the path.

Collecting features To avoid walking too far, use features that tell you when you have passed your destination e.g. a wall, steep ground or flat ground.

Hand railing Follow an obvious feature – a cliff edge, stream or wall.

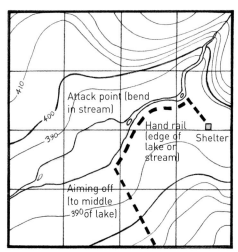

Fig. 41 Hand-railing, attack point and aiming off

If, after following one of the previous techniques and checking your map for obvious features, you cannot find what you are looking for, you must conduct a systematic search to locate your next point. There are two types of search you can undertake:

1 SPIRAL SEARCH (Fig. 42)
Good if you are alone:

- Use your compass and walk north to the limit of your visibility. Stop and turn 90° to the right and walk twice the limit of your visibility (you will have to pace accurately).
- Stop again and turn another 90° and walk three times the limit of your visibility.
- Keep repeating this process with longer and longer legs until you find your checkpoint or object.

2 SWEEP SEARCH
The more people the better for this approach:

- Space everyone out, but remain within sight, and sweep backwards and forwards across the area until your checkpoint or object is located.
- To work out the limit of visibility distance, ask someone to pace away from you. Stop them when it becomes difficult to see them – this is your distance.

SEARCH AND RELOCATION

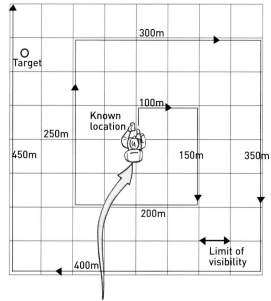

***Fig. 42** Spiral search*

EXPERT TIP

**Lorenz Frutiger IFMGA
Mountain Guide**
www.expeditiongreenland.com

'The story about the tortoise and hare often holds true; a party moving steadily the entire day will be faster than the party that 'runs' between long breaks.'

A GPS:

- Picks up signals from satellites.
- Calculates your position and displays it as a latitude and longitude fixed to the nearest 1/100th of a minute or as a grid reference.
- Gives the direction, the speed at which you are moving, the distance to a location and the altitude.

The receiver needs to pick up signals from at least three satellites – more satellites provide greater accuracy. Like any other position measuring device, a GPS isn't perfect. Officially, positioning with 95 per cent confidence will be accurate to better than 20m, but in effect it will often be much better than that.

Fig. 43 Study the instructional manual for your model carefully. An excellent resource for novice GPS usage is available on www.Garmin.com.

Fig. 44 *A GPS is useful in poorly mapped areas (trekking in Peru).*

GPS AND MAPS

When relating the position given by a GPS to a map a problem arises. Different countries have their own datum in which their country is mapped – if your GPS is not set to the right one, it can place you as much as several hundred metres off route.

There are dozens of selectable datum pre-loaded into a GPS so that it can be used anywhere in the world. In 1984, a world geodetic survey was published and it is now possible to produce maps and charts of the Earth's surface to a common datum – WGS84. Many countries are converting their maps to the WGS84 datum.

PROBLEMS WITH GPS

A GPS can provide very accurate information but, for mountain navigation, it is only an aid; traditional map and compass skills remain the backbone of sound navigation. Relying solely on a GPS would be foolish, considering:

- The batteries can run flat.
- There are still times when GPS can give a bad position without warning.
- Users of GPS in high northern latitudes will receive signals from satellites at relatively low elevations to the south of them. These may then be obscured by steep ground.
- A signal error may occur if the receiver is close to large reflective objects such as boulders or cliffs.
- Severe weather conditions can prevent you from operating your GPS – pressing small buttons while wearing gloves and reading the screen in a storm can be difficult.

ADVANTAGES OF GPS

A GPS is an aid in complex and featureless terrain, where traditional map-and-compass navigation is tricky e.g. crossing ice caps or a poorly mapped area. It can:

- Give a very accurate grid reference of your present location.
- Provide the facility to return to within a few metres of a previously visited location by marking a 'waypoint' at the location (useful in bad weather).
- Allow you to enter the grid reference of a specific point you want to go to.
- Show you the bearing and distance to the next objective, but when a GPS unit indicates you are 1 mile from a designated spot, that is an 'as the crow flies' mile, not a mountain mile.
- Track positions all day for later comparison with the map.
- Link with digital maps to upload waypoints or routes, email waypoints to friends and download your track to a map.

DON'T FORGET!

When following a 'GO TO' direction on a GPS, it is very easy to ignore the ground under your feet, to leave the map in your pocket and to forget about the contours. You can get into a situation where you are lost, relying solely on only your GPS, and at the mercy of technology.

SEARCH AND RELOCATION

An **altimeter** measures atmospheric pressure just like a barometer and turns it into an estimation of altitude, using either a dial with a needle or a digital display. Since the weather is caused by high and low pressure systems, you must regularly calibrate the altimeter by setting it when you are at a known elevation. An altimeter not only shows the advancing low pressure sysem, but it can also be used for navigation:

- Knowing your exact altitude can help you to pinpoint your position, especially on large uniform slopes and ridges.

- Altimeters can be more useful than a map in poor visibility or places where a map is not of much use such as a rock climb.

- Altimeters are particularly useful when accurately following a contour line for any distance.

- They help you descend and ascend to a specific point (note the target altitude from the map, but 'aim high' when coming down from above and 'aim low' when coming up from below). You can even set your altimeter alarm.

- Combined with slope aspect an altimeter can position you more accurately.

- It can help with planning ahead e.g. how much height is left to reach a summit? Have you reached the summit? How far down is halfway?

- You can monitor your progress through the day – if it has taken 1 hour to climb the first 400m and you have another 700m to go, then you can expect it to take at least 2 more hours to get there.

ALTIMETER LIMITATIONS
The Pressure Graph
Air pressure does not decrease uniformly as you ascend, but altimeters approximate that it does over small ranges. Reset it to a new reference altitude after changes in height of several hundred metres.

Weather changes
Small changes in air pressure significantly change the altitude reading, so recalibrate every few hours.

Temperature effects
The altimeter uses a list of average air temperatures for different altitudes. The problem is that the air temperature in your location is unlikely to be exactly the world average for that particular altitude. Regularly set the altitude at known points to minimise any effects. In cold weather (below 15°C at sea level/freezing level of 2400m) an altimeter tends to under-read any altitude changes. Conversely in hot weather, it tends to over-read changes.

Wind effects
An increase in wind speed due to air flowing around an object creates a drop in pressure where the wind speed is highest. Conversely, if you set the altimeter out of the wind, and then use it somewhere much windier, it might read too high.

Scrambling is the link between mountain walking and rock climbing, and is potentially a hazardous activity involving efficient movement in exposed terrain. You must make judgements continuously, not only about the terrain ahead, but also about both your own and your partners' ability.

Note: If you do not understand terms such as creating a belay, anchors, belaying etc., then read the *Rucksack Guide: Rock Climbing* **(A&C Black, 2009) first.**

The amount of equipment depends on the grade of the scramble:

- For simple scrambles you may only require a 30m single rope tied around the waist, a sling and an HMS krab. For more difficult scrambles you require a full rock climbing rack and a 50m single rope.

- Good footwear is essential – a stiff boot with no lateral twist provides a solid foundation.

- Leather gloves improve your grip on the rope when moving together and short roping.

- Routes are usually on high mountains and rucksacks with standard safety equipment for summer trekking are usually carried.

CLIMBING RACK FOR DIFFICULT SCRAMBLES

One set of nuts	2 x 120 slings
Hexes 4–8	4 x extenders
Friends 1, 2, 3	4 x screwgate krabs
2 x 240cm slings	2 x HMS krabs

Techniques are divided into the different standards of terrain encountered on a scramble:

WALKING TERRAIN
Ask yourself what the consequences of a fall are and what the terrain ahead is like. Is there more walking after the difficult step or do you need to rope-up? Do you require a harness or can you attach the rope around the waist? What are your partner's abilities? Are you both stable on your feet? Are you climbers or walkers? Your answers to these questions should tell you if you have moved on to the next level of terrain (p. 103).

SPOTTING
Spotting is an essential skill when the rock steps are not difficult and the consequences of a slip are not serious. Spotters do not catch falling climbers; they steer them to the best landing, slow them down and minimise the number of body parts hitting the ground. The size and skill of the spotter, the landing quality, plus the scrambler's height above the ground all determine the seriousness of the rock step. Consider using two spotters if the climber is large.

- When the rock step is steep, grab the sides of the climber's back just below the armpits and swing them back to a feet-first landing.
- As they get higher, spot the climber's hips and steer them to a feet-first landing, but do not grab them too low, as this may cause them to topple backwards.
- The falling climber must try to keep their limbs relaxed and land feet-first.

SCRAMBLING

Fig. 45 *Walking terrain. A rope is not required, but you must be able to 'spot' each other on a difficult step.*

ADVICE FOR SPOTTING

- Stop finger injuries – take care if you are wearing a climbing harness.
- Remove jewellery.
- Stand in a karate or boxing stance, braced, ready to support a falling climber.
- Keep your arms at the ready and not down by your side.
- Keep your arms close to the climber.
- Keep your fingers together so they do not bend back.

EASY CLIMBING TERRAIN [Fig. 46]
This type of terrain brings difficult and exposed steps where a slip is serious and spotting may no longer be effective. Use the rope and move together using a technique commonly called **short roping**. As soon as you are on ground that you would rather pitch, i.e. on a rock climb, but decide to move together and place protection, it becomes simu-climbing (see *Rucksack Guide: Alpinism* [A&C Black, 2009]).

The art of moving together using short roping requires fluency and concentration and a good body stance. It is a difficult skill to do smoothly and safely, and practice on non-dangerous terrain is essential.

SCRAMBLING

Fig. 46 *Easy climbing terrain. Spotting alone is not enough and requires use of short roping technique.*

The number of people on one rope depends on the terrain, weather, and the scrambler's size, weight, skill and experience. Generally three people are a maximum.

Method one

This is the most versatile method:

- The most experienced scrambler ties into the rope, and takes chest coils leaving about two/three arm lengths to the next scrambler.

- The last scrambler ties into the end of the rope and takes a coil around their chest to allow for extension on difficult sections (Fig. 48).

- The second scrambler attaches two arm spans in front of the rear scrambler via a loop created using an alpine butterfly or an overhand knot (avoid long loops that hang around the knees). The second scrambler ties into the rope loop using a rewoven overhand knot.

● This method of attaching two scramblers allows tension to be given to them individually or together.

Fig. 47 Attaching two people to the rope: (1) Alpine butterfly or overhand knot and a re-threaded overhand creating an isolation loop (2) Normal tie-in (loops shorten the rope giving extra distance when needed).

Method two

- The 'V' method of attachment is where each scrambler is attached to an end and the leader is tied into the middle or the two other ends. It has the advantage that it is easier to maintain tension on individual scramblers. It can also be used in descent.

- Problems can occur when descending broken ground, as the scramblers must take different lines to avoid the rope getting in the way of each other.

- It is also more difficult to use when traversing.

SHORTENING THE ROPE

- The full length of the rope is rarely required. Tie into the end and shorten it by taking chest coils (Fig. 48).

- Ensure the coils are long enough to reach 10cm above the top of your harness, and remember to wear them on the outside of your rucksack to enable you to drop them quickly.

- Taking three separate sets of tied-off coils allows you to drop one without the bother of retying the remaining coils.

- The disadvantage of multiple coils is the number of knots left at your waist.

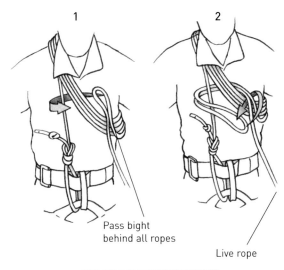

Pass bight
behind all ropes

Live rope

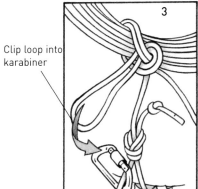

Clip loop into
karabiner

Fig. 48 *Shortening the rope by taking coils*

EXPERT TIP

**Louise Thomas
BMG/IFMGA Mountain
Guide**
Twid_turner@aol.com
www.sheersummits. com

'The rope is no use in the
bottom of your rucksack.
It is best carried uncoiled
in a stuff sac, with the end
protruding out of the lid
for easy access.'

HOLDING THE ROPE
Before looking at the skill of short roping you need to
learn the different methods of holding the rope. When
short roping the leader must hold the rope to the two
scramblers behind, adjusting the tension continuously
to keep the rope taut. There are a number of methods:

No coils in your hand (Fig. 49)
Hold the rope with your little finger closest to the
downhill scramblers (Fig. 49). You can also tie a
trucker's hitch in the rope and hold it just in front of
the hitch (Fig. 50). This is useful when it is cold or if
you have small hands. The disadvantage is that as the
terrain changes, you must constantly release and redo
the knot.

Fig. 49 Holding the rope without coils, little finger down the rope.

Fig. 50 Holding the rope with a slipknot

Coils in hand (Fig. 51)

Take coils in one hand and lock them off with a final twist around the palm, or lap the rope across the palm with one final twist. Both free the other hand, but prevent the coils being released under tension.

Fig. 51 Locking coils

Using both hands

Take coils in one hand (Fig. 51), but hold the rope to the climbers in the other. The tension can then be released if a belay is required. The disadvantage is that both hands are occupied.

Moving together/short roping

- At all times ask, 'Can I hold my partner should they slip?' If you cannot, do something about it!

- Place the weakest member next to the leader, if there is risk of a serious slip.

- The leader should always be above their partners whenever possible.

- On traverses, carry the rope in the downhill hand and stay directly above your partner. It is better for the leader to be on the uphill side of the rope, and for the rope running from the last scrambler to be on the downhill side of the next scrambler.

- When there are two scramblers behind you on a traverse, hold the rope between the two climbers. If you cannot be above them, then stay as close together as the terrain allows, because the rope's elasticity makes it harder to arrest a slip the further apart you are.

- Move any loose rock if there is a chance you could knock it down on to a following party.

- When you come to a section where you or your partner cannot maintain a stable base, stop. Climb over the difficulty and then continue as before.

- Do not run-out long lengths of rope unless you are going to set up a belay, because communication becomes difficult.

- On an easy ridge, the last climber on the rope can take a few coils in their hands. This gives them a few seconds' thought before deciding which side of the ridge to step on if someone falls. It may necessitate lengthening the rope between the climbers.

● When the ridge becomes more difficult it is more appropriate to pitch it, or to move together with runners between the leader and climbers (simu climbing).

MINIMISING BEING PULLED OFF-BALANCE
● Keep your movements regular.
● Keep your arm slightly bent to act as a clutch and absorb some of the initial force in a slip.
● When this is not possible, take the rope in and pay it out as your pace varies.
● Be alert for spikes and boulders around which to loop the rope.
● Look ahead for problem steps and possible belays.

MORE DIFFICULT CLIMBING TERRAIN
Varies from a single short section of difficulty on an otherwise easy scramble, to a full rock climb. You are now no longer confident that a slip can be held while moving together, and the consequences of a fall are serious. Use methods similar to rock climbing:

1 **Attach the scrambler/s to the rock** Wrap the rope around a boulder, drape the rope between them over a spike, or clip the rope between the scramblers into a belay.

2 **The leader then climbs the pitch** Belayed or not, placing protection if required (*see Rucksack Guide: Rock Climbing* (2008)).

3 **The seconds must then be belayed up the climb**. This can vary from a full rock climbing belay (usually a direct one) to a braced stance (*see* Belays, pp. 116–8).

When the section is long or the consequences of a fall are more serious, e.g. a fall would leave the seconds hanging in space, consider placing runners in the pitch, even if the leader does not require them.

DIRECT AND INDIRECT BELAYING

Direct and indirect belaying describes how the forces created in a fall reach the belay anchors.

A **direct belay** transmits the forces direct to the belay anchors. The belayer is free to move around, and lowering, sorting hoists and holding a fall are easier. It should, however, not be used to belay a lead climber.

An **indirect belay** transmits the forces to the belay anchors via the belayer e.g. waist belay. The body absorbs some of the forces and the belayer can feel the climber's movement.

A **semi-direct belay system** is used by most climbers, because the forces are transmitted direct to the anchors, but by changing position the belayer can also absorb the force.

FALLING OBJECTS

Should anything fall down the crag, do not look up to see where it is coming from – it may be closer than you would wish. Instead, when you hear a shout, run towards the cliff. Falling objects do not normally fall straight down the rock face: they usually bounce out a few feet.

Fig. 52 *More difficult scrambling terrain. The belayer in this photograph must be absolutely sure that a leader fall is not going to pull him upwards.*

BELAYS REQUIRING THE ROPE ONLY

If there is a chance the scramblers may have to be lowered back down, might swing into space or may both slip at the same time, the methods below are unsuitable:

Braced stance behind a boulder (Fig. 53)

If the boulder is low down, sit behind it and use a waist belay.

Fig. 53 Waist belaying braced behind a boulder – not to be used when there is chance of a serious fall.

Direct belay (Fig. 54)

Pull the rope around a spike or boulder. Whether you need to be attached depends on the size of the stance.

Combination belay

Take the rope around a boulder and waist belay.

Fig. 54 *Direct belay on a flake – again, not suitable when there is a chance of a serious fall.*

BELAYS WHEN A FALL IS SERIOUS

When choosing a belay you should try to match the seriousness of the situation to the type of belay used and the distance the climbers are away from you. Apply the same factors for selecting anchors and creating a belay as you would when rock climbing – choose solid, equalised and independent anchors, and consider the direction a fall will pull you in, the tension on the belay and your ability to communicate with other climbers.

The size of the stance determines whether the leader is also attached to the belay:

- Place a sling through a thread, or over a spike/boulder, and direct belay to it using an Italian hitch or Petzl Reverso.
- Place runner/s, equalise them with slings and direct belay to it using an Italian hitch or Reverso.

It is often difficult to work out how the force created in a fall will be transmitted to the belay/er, especially on a ridge, because the climber may slip and pendulum sideways. If there is a traverse, ensure you are above it or have placed runners to protect it, or there are boulders and spikes to catch a falling climber.

When the climbers arrive at the stance, attach individually via a locking krab, or by clipping the rope between them into the belay or over a spike to counterbalance them.

DESCENDING METHODS

The method you use depends on the size and experience of the scramblers plus the steepness and condition of the descent.

Easiest line

● Choose the easiest line for the leader to protect the scrambler below. This may not necessarily be the same as the easiest line for the scramblers. Can you hold a slip or do you need to lower the lead scramblers down the section or even to abseil?

Placing feet

● Inform the lead scramblers as often as necessary when you want them to stop for you to place your feet properly on difficult ground.

Tension in the rope

● Ensure you maintain tension in the rope and, if the ground is difficult, place runners to protect the rear scrambler.

Facing out

● When the terrain is difficult, down climbing, facing in, feels secure but makes the terrain below look harder than it is. Facing out is faster but less secure.

● When it becomes too difficult, lower one scrambler, who places protection or abseil.

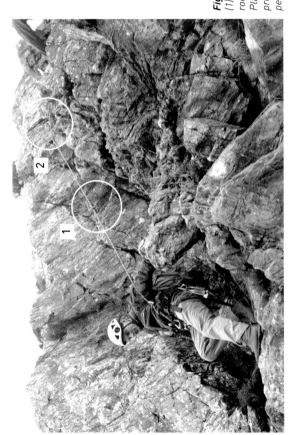

Fig. 55 Descending (1) Using a natural rock feature (2) Placing a runner to protect the last person descending

MOUNTAIN ROUTES

Via ferrata are mountain routes equipped with fixed cables, ladders and bridges. They break just about every rule of aesthetic mountaineering, but they provide an opportunity to move through spectacular and often extremely exposed alpine scenery with minimal equipment.

The routes are generally technically straight-forward for a competent climber, but they are steep, exposed and can be very strenuous. It may be appropriate for some parties to carry a rope and to be able to direct belay and set up a pulley system.

Grading

In the Dolomite Mountains, Italy, routes are graded according to their difficulty.

Grade one usually involves nothing more than an assisted walk.

Grade five demands serious climbing skills.

Another system uses numbers 1–5 indicating the technical difficulty and letters A, B or C indicating the overall commitment and seriousness level.

See www.viaferrata.org for more information. Even for climbers with technical climbing skills and alpine mountaineering experience there are some dangers that cannot be avoided:

- Loose rock
- Corroded or missing ladder rungs or fixings – be vigilant and test doubtful rungs before placing all your weight on them.
- Damaged wire ropes – wear tough gloves to protect against broken strands.
- Missing protection on older routes – ask locals or consider carrying a rope and climbing gear.
- The weather – carry waterproofs if rain is likely.
- Lightning – in a thunderstorm get away from iron ladders and wire ropes (this may mean abseiling off the route)!

EQUIPMENT
- A **helmet** is advisable.
- **Footwear** should not be soft-soled.
- **Gloves** are useful.
- A **harness and shock absorbing system** is vital.
- Take a **jumper, first aid kit, water** and **head torch**.

SHOCK ABSORBERS
There are no circumstances in which you should attempt a Via ferrata using climbing slings without a Kinetic Impact Shock Absorber (KISA), because a fall can shock-load the slings beyond their breaking strength (Fig. 56). A Via ferrata system comprises a length of dynamic rope threaded through a KISA which leads to a rope or tape Y, with a Klettersteig karabiner at the end of each arm (they offer protection if both arms of the lanyard are clipped into the cable).

OLDER SYSTEMS

Older metal shock absorbers suffer from a major limitation – it is essential to be clipped into one arm only if you fall. If both arms are clipped on to the cable and you fall, the energy absorber won't work. If using this type of shock absorber, take extra care when moving past an intermediate anchor point.

***Fig. 56** A Petzl Scorpio Vertigo KISA – never attempt a Via ferrata without one.*

Via ferrata systems

Some Via ferrata systems also have a short third arm, which allows you to rest on steep sections. Check there is a 'K' in a circle on the spine of the krab attached to the ends – if there is an 'H' in a circle it is an HMS karabiner for belaying, and is not designed for Via ferrata use. Most modern lanyards are larks footed onto the abseil loop of the harness.

***Fig. 57** Are Via ferrata safe? As with all in situ equipment don't blindly trust any of the metal. Take a look at www.viaferrata.org.*

Shock absorber technique [Fig. 58]

- Both karabiners should be attached to the cable at all times, unless you are passing an anchor point.
- If you fall on a horizontal section, you won't go anywhere. If you fall on a vertical or diagonal section, you'll slide down to the last anchor!
- The 'shock absorber' will keep you, the rope and the cable from receiving too great a shock.
- If you become tired take a rest using the short sling.

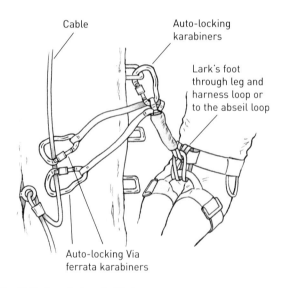

Cable

Auto-locking karabiners

Lark's foot through leg and harness loop or to the abseil loop

Auto-locking Via ferrata karabiners

Fig. 58 *Basic technique for Via ferrata*

WEATHER FORECAST SOURCES

Source	Pros	Cons
National radio/TV forecasts	Some local stations provide special mountain forecasts, but of course you must be in the area to receive it.	Mostly too general and do not tell you what is happening to developing depressions.
Weather maps	A good way to get information and you can take them with you.	Newspapers often use the previous day's weather map.
Telephone /fax	With access to a fax machine you can obtain a detailed forecast plus an Atlantic chart from the UK Met Office.	There are many premium rate services, but they are costly as you listen to information you don't need.
Internet	You can take your time, print maps out and you have access to web cams all over the world showing real-time weather.	You must be able to link up and have a decent connection. Not all sites are reliable.

UK scrambles are usually rated using Steve Ashton's system of grades 1, 2, 3 or 3S (S for serious), with the grade being based around technical difficulty, the need to use a rope and exposure.

GRADE	DETAIL
Grade 1	Straightforward for experienced hill walkers. It may be necessary to use the hands occasionally for progress. The exposure is not too daunting.
Grade 2	This grade is more sustained and requires more use of the hands. The exposure is significant and retreat difficult.
Grade 3	The rock becomes very steep and is exposed at times. Most people will prefer a rope, and there are occasional moves more akin to a full rock climb. The ability to abseil may be important.

Some books on scrambling rate the routes:

LEVEL	DETAIL
Easy	Just off-trail hiking with minimal exposure (if at all), and perhaps a handhold or two. UIAA Class I.
Moderate	Handholds frequently needed, possible exposure, route-finding skills helpful. UIAA Class II.
Difficult	Almost constant handholds, fall distance may be fatal, route finding-skills needed, loose and down-sloping rock. Less experienced parties may consider using a rope for short sections.

In the US, the Yosemite Decimal System (YDS) is used. The system consists of five classes indicating the technical difficulty of the hardest section:

CLASS	DETAIL
Class 1	Walking with a low chance of injury or fatality
Classes 2 and 3	Steeper routes with increased exposure and a greater chance of severe injury, but falls are not always fatal
Class 4	Can involve short, steep sections where the use of a rope is recommended, and un-roped falls could be fatal
Class 5	Considered true rock climbing, predominantly on vertical or near vertical rock

ROCK CLIMBING

Rock climbing can be a tough, sometimes dangerous, physical and mental challenge. This book covers everything you need to know to be safe when ascending steep rock formations, including belaying, aid climbing and how to learn to move efficiently.

MOUNTAINEERING IN REMOTE AREAS OF THE WORLD

This is the essential handbook for planning and undertaking mountaineering expeditions around the world. It offers concise guidance, including where to go and when, advice on dangerous animals and minimising your impact on the environment, and dealing with extreme situations.

ALPINISM

Venturing to the Alps for the first time can be daunting. This volume covers everything you need to know about ascending these magnificent mountains, in summer and winter.

SKI MOUNTAINEERING AND SNOWSHOEING

Mountaineering on skis or snowshoes requires the ability to ski off-piste, good navigation skills, and awareness of the risks of the mountain environment in winter – you will find all of the above and more covered in this handbook.

WINTER MOUNTAINEERING

Mountains transformed by snow and ice are a world apart from lush summer slopes. This volume provides you with the techniques to explore wintry plateaus, tackle rocky ridges and ascend snowy slopes.